YOUR SORROW WILL TURN TO JOY

MORNING & EVENING
MEDITATIONS
OR HOLY WEEK

Published by Desiring God
Post Office Box 2901
Minneapolis, MN 55402
www.desiringGod.org

Cover design and typesetting
Taylor Design Works

TABLE OF CONTENTS

CONTRIBUTORS

Jon Bloom is author, board chair, and co-founder of desiringGod.org. He is author of *Not by Sight*, *Things Not Seen*, and *Don't Follow Your Heart*. He lives in Minneapolis with his wife, Pam, and their five children.

Johnathan Bowers is instructor of theology and Christian worldview at Bethlehem College & Seminary in Minneapolis, Minnesota. He is a PhD candidate in Christian philosophy at Southern Baptist Theological Seminary. He lives in Minneapolis with his wife, Crystal, and their son.

Andreas Köstenberger is senior research professor of New Testament and biblical theology at Southeastern Baptist Theological Seminary in Wake Forest, North Carolina. He is co-author with Justin Taylor of *The Final Days of Jesus: The Most Important Week of the Most Important Person Who Ever Lived*.

David Mathis is executive editor for desiringGod.org, adjunct professor with Bethlehem College & Seminary, and pastor at Cities Church, Minneapolis. He is author of *Habits of Grace: Enjoying Jesus through the Spiritual Disciplines* and lives in Minneapolis with his wife, Megan, and their three children.

Donald Macleod was professor of systematic theology at the Free Church of Scotland College in Edinburgh for more than thirty years. He is author of *The Person of Christ* and most recently *Christ Crucified*.

Jonathan Parnell is the lead pastor of Cities Church. He lives in St. Paul with his wife, Melissa, and their five children. He is coauthor of *How to Stay Christian in Seminary* and author of the forthcoming *Glory and Gladness*.

John Piper is founder and teacher for desiringGod.org and chancellor for Bethlehem College & Seminary. For more than thirty years, he served as pastor of Bethlehem Baptist Church. He is author of more than fifty books, and his sermons, articles, and books are available free of charge at desiringGod.org. John and his wife, Nöel, have four sons, one daughter, and twelve grandchildren.

Tony Reinke is a staff writer for desiringGod.org and host of the popular podcast *Ask Pastor John*. He is author of *Lit! A Chrisitan Guide to Reading Books*, *John Newton on the Christian Life*, and *The Joy Project*. He lives in the Twin Cities with his wife, Karaleigh, and their three children.

Joe Rigney is assistant professor of theology and Christian worldview at Bethlehem College & Seminary. He is author of *The Things of Earth: Treasuring God by Enjoying His Gifts* and lives in Minneapolis with his wife, Jenny, and two sons.

Marshall Segal is associate editor for desiringGod.org and executive assistant to John Piper. He is a graduate of Bethlehem College & Seminary and lives in Minneapolis with his wife, Faye.

Justin Taylor is senior vice president and publisher for books at Crossway and an elder at New Covenant Bible Church in St. Charles, Illinois. He and his wife, Lea, have four children. He is co-author with Andreas Köstenberger of *The Final Days of Jesus: The Most Important Week of the Most Important Person Who Ever Lived*.

Truly, truly, I say to you,
you will weep and lament,
but the world will rejoice.
You will be sorrowful,
but your sorrow will turn into joy.

JOHN 16:20

PREFACE

In one sense, there's nothing special about "Holy Week." Just another sequence of eight days each spring—nothing is intrinsically holy about this Sunday to Sunday that moves around the calendar each year.

We have no mandate from Jesus or his apostles to mark these days for particular observance. Paul, for one, would be quite happy for us to partake, or not. "One person esteems one day as better than another, while another esteems all days alike. Each one should be fully convinced in his own mind" (Rom. 14:5). Clearly, the celebration should not be pressed upon the conscience of others. "Let no one pass judgment on you in questions of food and drink, or with regard to a festival or a new moon or a Sabbath" (Col. 2:16).

Marking Holy Week is not an obligation, but it is an opportunity. It is a chance to walk with the church, throughout time and through the world, as she walks with her Bridegroom through the most important week in the history of the world. It is a chance to focus our minds on, and seek to intensify our affections for, the most important and timeless realities.

While not mandating the observance, or even suggesting it, the New Testament does give us (indirect) reason, if we're looking for it. The final eight of Matthew's 28 chapters are given to this one week, along with the last six of Mark's sixteen and the final six of Luke's 24. Most significant, though, is John. Ten of the Gospel's 21 chapters—essentially half—deal with the final week of our Lord's life, his betrayal, his trials, his crucifixion, and his triumphant resurrection. Even Acts, which then narrates the life of the early church, returns to the events of Holy Week with frequency (see, for instance, Acts 1:15–19; 2:22–36; 3:11–26; 4:8–12, 24–28, among others). Indeed, it could even be said that all the Old Testament anticipates this week, and the rest of the New Testament reflects it in theology and practical living.

To help with the opportunity Holy Week presents, we have assembled a team of eleven pastors and scholars to walk us through Holy Week as we walk together with our Lord. The book you're holding includes relatively brief readings for each morning and evening for the eight days of Holy Week, from Palm Sunday to Easter.

We encourage you to slow down and savor these meditations. Meditate on the truths in these meditations. Perhaps block out several minutes. Find a comfortable place to sit. Quiet your soul, and pray that God would meet you in these words. Consider spending a few moments in prayer after you read and turn these truths Godward in adoration of Christ.

In the chaos of our increasingly fast-paced and hectic society, Holy Week is a reminder to pause and ponder, to carefully mark each day and not let this greatest of all weeks fly by us like every other.

Our prayer for you as you read is that God would make the apostle's prayer in Ephesians 3:16–19 come true in you this Holy Week:

> *that according to the riches of his glory he may grant you to be strengthened with power through his Spirit in your inner being, so that Christ may dwell in your hearts through faith—that you, being rooted and grounded in love, may have strength to comprehend with all the saints what is the breadth and length and height and depth, and to know the love of Christ that surpasses knowledge, that you may be filled with all the fullness of God.*

May it truly be a week for being newly grounded in the love of Christ, which is so plainly on display from the resolve of Palm Sunday, to the ultimate sacrifice of Good Friday, to the triumph of Easter Sunday. And may you freshly know the love of Christ, in all its breadth and length and height and depth—and wonder upon wonder, be filled with all the fullness of God.

Special thanks to Bryan DeWire for his help in pulling these meditations together in this form for publication, and for the observation above about how many chapters of the Gospel accounts are dedicated to Holy Week.

David Mathis
Executive Editor
desiringGod.org

PALM

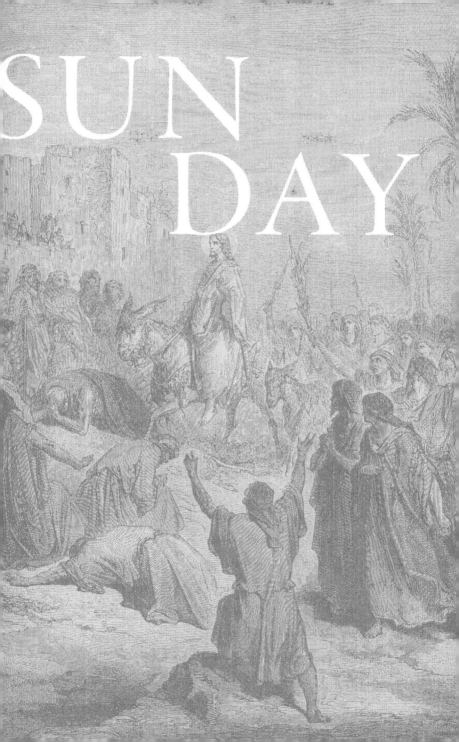

SUN DAY

THE SAVIOR'S TEARS OF SOVEREIGN MERCY

John Piper

> *"Hosanna! Blessed is he who comes in the name of the Lord! Blessed is the coming kingdom of our father David! Hosanna in the highest!" (Mark 11:9–10)*

Palm Sunday is the day in the church year when tradition-ally we mark the entrance of Jesus into Jerusalem for the last week of his life.

As he rode into town on the humble beast, Jesus was not oblivious to what was about to happen to him. His enemies were going to get the upper hand, and he would be rejected and crucified. And within a generation the city would be obliterated. Here's how Jesus says it in Luke 19:43–44:

> *"The days will come upon you, when your enemies will set up a barricade around you and surround you and hem you in on every side and tear you down to the*

ground, you and your children within you. And they will not leave one stone upon another in you, because you did not know the time of your visitation."

God was visiting them in Jesus, his Son—"he came to his own, and his own received him not" (John 1:11). But they did not know the time of their visitation. So they stumbled over the stumbling stone. The builders rejected the stone and threw it away. Jesus saw this coming.

The King Cries

How did he respond? "When he drew near and saw the city, he wept over it, saying, 'Would that you, even you, had known on this day the things that make for peace! But now they are hidden from your eyes'" (Luke 19:41–42). Jesus wept over the blindness and the impending misery of Jerusalem.

How would you describe these tears? I would call them *tears of sovereign mercy.* The effect they should have on us is to make us admire Christ and treasure him above all others and worship him as our merciful Sovereign. And when we have seen the beauty of his mercy, we become merciful with him and like him and for his glory.

So, let's admire Christ together on this Palm Sunday.

Admiring His Tender Sovereignty

What makes Christ so admirable and so different than all other persons is that he unites in himself so many qualities that in other people are contrary to each other. We can imagine supreme sovereignty, and we can imagine tenderhearted mercy. But to whom do we look to combine, in perfect proportion, merciful sovereignty and sovereign mercy? We look to Jesus. No other religious or political contender even comes close.

Look at three pointers to his sovereignty in the Palm Sunday account.

First, the crowds praised God for Jesus's mighty works (Luke 19:37). He had healed leprosy with a touch; he had made the blind see and the deaf hear and the lame walk; he had commanded the unclean spirits and they obeyed him; he had stilled storms and walked on water and turned five loaves and two fish into a meal for thousands. So as he entered Jerusalem, they knew nothing could stop him. He could just speak and Pilate would perish; the Romans would be scattered. He was sovereign.

Then look, secondly, at verse 38. The crowds cried out, "Blessed is the King who comes in the name of the Lord!" Jesus was a King, and not just any king, but the one sent and appointed by the Lord God. They knew how Isaiah had described him—as sovereign over an invincible, never-ending kingdom:

Of the increase of his government and of peace there will be no end, on the throne of David and over his kingdom, to establish it and to uphold it with justice and with righteousness from this time forth and forevermore. The zeal of the Lord of hosts will do this. (Isa. 9:7)

A universal, never-ending kingdom backed by the zeal of almighty God. Here was the King of the universe, who today rules over the nations and the galaxies, and for whom America and ISIS and every other political state are only a grain of sand and a vapor.

Third, verse 40. When the Pharisees tell him to make the people stop blessing him as a king, he answers, "I tell you, if these were silent, the very stones would cry out" (Luke 19:40). Why? Because Jesus *will* be praised! The whole design of the universe is that Christ be praised. And therefore, if people won't do it, he will see to it that rocks do it.

In other words, he is sovereign. He will get what he means to get. If we refuse to praise, the rocks will get the joy.

Fulfillment, Not Failure

It is remarkable, therefore, that the tears of Jesus in verse 41 are so often used to deny his sovereignty. Someone will say, "Look, he weeps over Jerusalem because his design for them is not coming to pass. He would delight in their salvation. But they are resistant. They are going to reject him. They are going to hand him over to be crucified. And so his purpose for them has failed." But there is something not quite right about this objection to Jesus's sovereignty.

He can make praise come from rocks. And so he could do the same from rock-hard hearts in Jerusalem. What's more, all this rejection and persecution and killing of Jesus are not the failure of Jesus's plan, but the fulfillment of it.

Listen to what he said in Luke 18:31–33 a short time before:

And taking the twelve, he said to them, "See, we are going up to Jerusalem, and everything that is written [planned!] about the Son of Man by the prophets will be accomplished. For he will be delivered over to the

*Gentiles and will be mocked and shamefully treated
and spit upon. And after flogging him, they will kill
him, and on the third day he will rise."*

The betrayal, the mockery, the shame, the spit, the flogging, the murder—and so much more—was planned. In other words, the resistance, the rejection, the unbelief and hostility were not a surprise to Jesus. They were, in fact, part of the plan. He says so.

This is probably why it says at the end of verse 42, "But now they are hidden from your eyes." Remember what Jesus said about his parables in Luke 8:10: "To you [disciples] it has been given to know the secrets of the kingdom of God, but for others they are in parables, so that 'seeing they may not see, and hearing they may not understand.'" God was handing them over to hardness. It was judgment.

Merciful and Mighty

The mercy of God is a sovereign mercy. "I will have mercy on whom I have mercy, and I will have compassion on whom I have compassion" (Rom. 9:15). But here is the point we see on Palm Sunday: This sovereign Christ weeps over the hard-hearted, perishing people of Jerusalem as they fulfilled his plan. It is unbiblical and wrong to make the tears of mercy a contradiction to the serenity of sovereignty. Jesus was serene in sorrow, and sorrowful in sovereignty. Jesus's tears are the tears of sovereign mercy.

And therefore his sovereign power is the more admirable and the more beautiful. It's the harmony of things that seem in tension that makes him glorious—"merciful and mighty," as we sing. We admire power more when it is merciful power. And we admire mercy more when it is mighty mercy.

Oh that we would see and savor the beauty of Christ—the Palm Sunday tears of sovereign joy and the self-sacrificing love and obedience that took him every step of the way during Holy Week. And oh that as we admire and worship him this week we would be changed by what we see and become more tenderly-moved, self-denying, need-meeting people.

THE PROBLEM OF PALM SUNDAY

Jonathan Parnell

For centuries, the church has memorialized the first day of Holy Week as Palm Sunday because of the palm branches and cloaks that the people spread out before Jesus as he entered Jerusalem.

The Gospel writers tell us a crowd gathered, gushing with excitement, and lined the road in front of Jesus as he slowly rode into the city. As he made his way, one step at a time by the beast of burden on which he sat, a sort of carpet was being sewn together ahead of him. Fresh, green palm branches, presumably picked from nearby trees, and thick, worn clothing, likely from the backs of the crowd, formed a tapestry of endearment toward Israel's long-awaited Messiah.

And according to the Pharisees, this was a problem.

What the People Said

But actually, it wasn't the palm branches that were the problem so much as what the people were saying.

Luke tells us that as Jesus entered Jerusalem the people began rejoicing and praising God, shouting, "Blessed is the King who comes in the name of the Lord!" (Luke 19:38).

Some Pharisees try to get Jesus to make the crowd stop. They ask him to rebuke the people for what they're saying—the whole "Blessed is the King" bit.

The Pharisees get it, you see. This isn't just any phrase. This is the kind of welcome reserved for Israel's Savior.

It's a phrase found in the Hebrew Scriptures, going back to Psalm 118, a psalm that rejoices in the Lord's triumph. By verse 22 of this psalm, the rejected stone has become the "cornerstone" (Ps. 118:22). This is a marvelous work—by God's doing—which then launches the day of salvation (Ps. 118:23–24). This day of salvation is the long-anticipated deliverance that Israel thought might never come. But it will, it does, and Psalm 118:25 captures the hope: "Save us, we pray, O LORD! O LORD, we pray, give us success!"

Now this salvation and success is nothing generic. It will come through a person—the Messiah of God—the one sent to rescue his people. So goes the shout, in the psalm, "Blessed is he who comes in the name of the LORD!" (Ps. 118:26).

Without doubt, this rambling crowd in Jerusalem, taking its cues from Psalm 118, is declaring Jesus to be the Messiah. That's why the Pharisees tell Jesus to stop the madness. *Do you hear what they are saying? They think you're the Messiah come to save us. Tell them to shut up.*

Jesus doesn't stop them, though. He says, instead, that if the people weren't saying it, then the rocks themselves would cry out. Of course, Jesus is the Messiah. He has come to Jerusalem to save his people.

And according to the crowd, this was a problem.

What the People Saw

But actually, it wasn't the salvation part that was the problem so much as the way Jesus would bring salvation.

The people *wanted* salvation and success, remember. Which means, they wanted the Messiah to march into the city and do hard business with Rome. They wanted to be free from Gentile oppression, even if by force, even if by threats and plagues and a split sea, as they recounted so well in their history. They wanted another exodus, one that expelled the Romans.

Instead, what they got by Friday morning was a bloodied has-been, a man in Roman custody, rejected by their own leaders, standing next to an infamous criminal called Barabbas. They wanted an incomparable king, but they would see a beaten blasphemer. Or so they thought.

The sounds of the crowd this Palm Sunday would later be betrayed by the sounds of another crowd later that week. "Blessed is he!" would soon become "crucify him!" For this reason, there is something nauseating about today. We read of the response to Jesus, but because we know the story, we're aware that this thrilled welcome doesn't have the final say, at least not when it comes to the inhabitants of Jerusalem.

And as we feel the short-sighted joy of Sunday's words, their ineffective enthusiasm, we can't help but hear the railing that comes on Friday.

If we could listen in on these crowds, we'd hear our shouts along with theirs. We'd hear our praise, and then, by Friday, ashamed, we'd hear our mocking voice "call out among the scoffers." At some point in our lives, we've been part of both crowds. Maybe we would have praised him, but at some point we too have mocked.

It is not the righteous, after all, whom Jesus came to save, but sinners—like us.

HOLY

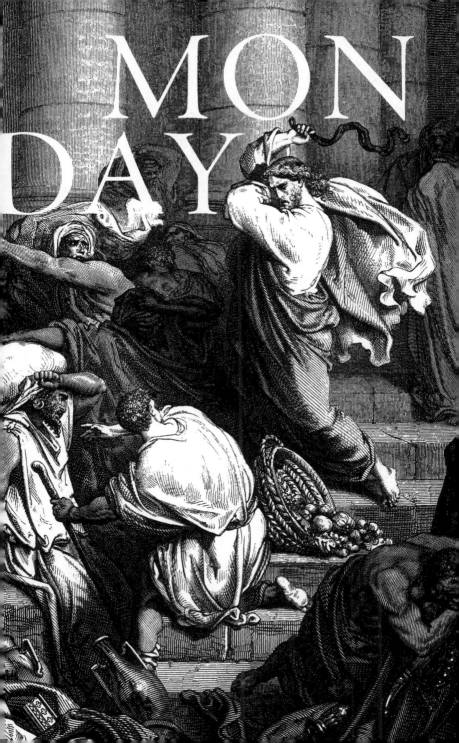

NO TURNING BACK

Andreas Köstenberger & Justin Taylor

The sun rises just before 6:30 A.M. in Bethany, the small village on the southeastern slope of the Mount of Olives, just a mile and a half east of Jerusalem. It is Monday morning, March 30, A.D. 33. Jesus of Nazareth is staying in the humble home of his friends Martha (whose anxiety-driven hospitality had received his gentle rebuke), Mary (who chose the good portion), and Lazarus (whose body would still be in the grave apart from the wonder-working of the Christ).

Just the day before—the first day of the last week of his life—Jesus had made his Triumphal Entry into the Holy City, riding on a donkey over a royal "red carpet" of palm branches and cloaks, hailed by his disciples and the Galilean pilgrims as the messianic king.

But Monday would be different than Sunday. Jesus knew the heart of man (John 2:24–25). He knew the acclaim of the disciples and the crowd was built on a messiah of their own imagination. Despite his many efforts at teaching them otherwise, they couldn't shake their wrong expectations. They were excited about a national savior who would overthrow the despised Romans once and for all. They had no categories for the idea that victory would come through *experiencing*, rather than inflicting, wrath and degrading shame.

Judgment Begins at Home

As Jesus and the Twelve awoke the next day, gathering at their appointed meeting place in Bethany to make their short trek back to Jerusalem, Jesus's agenda was the same as it remains today: to strip away misunderstandings of who he was and what he was going to accomplish so that our expectations could be confounded. This was not going to be a meek and mild Monday. Jesus was about to show them that judgment begins at home, with Israel.

As they walked together over the rocky terrain of the Mount of Olives, and as the hunger in Jesus's stomach grew, he spotted a fig tree off in the distance. From external appearances, it looked healthy, the perfect place to grab some fruit and to meet his need. But on closer inspection, the tree was barren of fruit, with nothing on it but inedible leaves.

The disciples could not have expected what Jesus did next. He called down a curse on the fig tree, declaring that it would never bear fruit again (Matt. 21:18–19; Mark 11:12–14). Jesus would expound on this visual parable tomorrow. But if the disciples were viewing the tree through spiritual eyes, they would remember that in the Old Testament, Israel was often referred to as a "fig tree" (Jer. 8:13; Hos. 9:10, 16; Joel 1:7). Judgment must begin at home.

Cleansing the Temple

They continued walking, the disciples undoubtedly unnerved by this unexpected behavior. But Jesus was just beginning.

When Jesus entered the Temple Mount later that day, he was surrounded by pious Jews who had made the pilgrimage to Jerusalem for Passover. Not only would they have to pay the Temple tax (a Tyrian shekel), but they would also have to purchase an unblemished sacrificial animal in the Court of the Gentiles. As Jesus looked at the moneychangers and merchants, a holy zeal and righteous indignation welled up within him. They were turning his Father's house of prayer for the nations (Isa. 56:7) into a den of thieves to prey upon the poor Passover pilgrims and to pervert true worship (Jer. 7:11). Jesus began overturning the tables and chairs of the moneychangers, throwing out the merchants and their scurrying customers, refusing entrance to any who carried goods for sale.

Face Like Flint

From the perspective of the chief priests, scribes, and Jewish leaders, it was one thing for this teacher from the backwaters of Nazareth to share his stories and make his claims and do his miracles with his followers. But now he was inside the Holy City. He had entered the gates like he was the new David or the new Solomon. And now he has the audacity to declare that the Temple in essence belongs to him and his Father? Who is he to suggest that the Jewish system was enabling sin rather than worship? And how dare he argue that the Jewish authorities were ignorant of true godliness and piety?

From this point forward, there would be no turning back. Jesus is not shrinking back. In fact, he is accelerating the sentence of death.

Evening approaches. The sun will set around 7:00 P.M., beginning the new day according to the Jewish calendar. Jesus and his disciples make their return to Bethany. Tomorrow will be a new day to confound, to turn things upside down, as Jesus continues to fulfill the eternal plan that will take him to Calvary.

JESUS TURNS THE TABLES

Jonathan Parnell

> *He entered the temple and began to drive out those*
> *who sold and those who bought in the temple, and he*
> *overturned the tables of the money-changers and the*
> *seats of those who sold pigeons. (Mark 11:15)*

This particular Monday may have felt like the proverbial Monday morning in the modern Western world—a time to reengage the grind and get back to work. Jesus, indeed, walked into Jerusalem to take care of business.

The meek and mild Jesus of progressive "tolerance" that so many of our contemporaries have come to prefer was nowhere to be found when he made a mess of the money-changers. There was nothing soft and tender on display when Jesus, in Jeremiah-like fashion, pronounced a resounding judgment on Israel.

In no uncertain terms, his rebuke fell on their worship.

Pigeons! Get Your Pigeons!

The Christian tradition in which I was raised regularly had visiting musical groups play concerts. As you can imagine, these groups would have their albums and other merchandise to promote on the circuit, but at our local church, they weren't allowed to sell them—at least not in the church foyer where most attenders entered. The rationale came from Mark 11:15–19 when Jesus cleansed the temple. *Jesus clearly didn't like it when folks hawked their wares around the temple, and therefore we shouldn't sell stuff around the sanctuary.*

To be sure, the place of worship in first-century Judaism and the auditorium of a rural Baptist church in America don't exactly correspond, but true to Jesus's words, my home church didn't want the place of worship to be co-opted as a place of commerce. And that much is right.

So this is one temple problem going on in Jesus's day. If you can imagine, the city would have been packed with pilgrims because of Passover. They would have come to the temple to offer sacrifices and, seizing an opportunity, pigeon-vendors set up shop. It might not have been too different from a sporting event today when sweaty salesmen walk the aisles and herald their popcorn—except these were sacrificial birds, their motive was sinister, and the prices were probably jacked even higher. "Pigeons! Get your pigeons!" they would have hollered.

Without doubt, this is a far cry from what the place of worship should have been, and Jesus wouldn't have it. Turning heads by his claim of authority, Jesus spoke for God and turned over tables. And central to it all was what he quoted from the Old Testament—from Isaiah and Jeremiah:

> *"Is it not written, 'My house shall be called a house of prayer for all the nations' [Isa. 56:7–8]? But you have made it a den of robbers [Jer. 7:11]."*

Out of Sync

The co-op for commerce was a problem, but that wasn't the only thing, or even the main thing, that Jesus was addressing. The real fiasco was how out of sync Israel's worship was with the great end-times vision Isaiah had prophesied—the new age that Jesus had come to inaugurate.

Jesus quotes a portion of that vision from Isaiah 56: "My house shall be called a house of prayer for all the nations."

The context of Isaiah 56 tells us more. According to Isaiah's vision, eunuchs would keep God's covenant (Isa. 56:4), and foreigners would join themselves to him (Isa. 56:6), and the outcasts would be gathered with his people (Isa. 56:8). But Jesus approached a temple pulsing with buying and selling. The court of the Gentiles, the place designed all along for foreigners to congregate, for the nations to seek the Lord, was overrun with opportunists trying to turn a profit. And the Jewish leaders had let this happen.

Their economic drive, and their false security in the temple as an emblem of blessing (Jer. 7:3–11), had crowded out space for the nations to draw near, and therefore Jesus was driving them out. The great sadness of this scene wasn't so much the rows of product and price-gouging, but that all this left no room for the Gentiles and outcasts to come to God. This place of worship should have prefigured the hope of God's restored creation—a day when "*all the nations* shall flow to it, and *many peoples* shall come, and say: 'Come, let us go to the mountain of the Lord, to the house of the God of Jacob'" (Isa. 2:2–3).

In other words, the ultimate vision of God's people in God's place would look a little more motley than it did when Jesus stepped foot into Jerusalem. And because their worship was so far removed from this vision, Jesus had enough. The worship of God's people was so out of line with God's purposes that zeal consumed God's Messiah. It had to stop.

What About Us?

And here is the lesson for us on this Monday of Holy Week, or really, here is the question: How well does our worship prefigure the prophetic vision of the new creation? Do our relational investments and our corporate gatherings reflect, even in a small way, the heart of a God who gathers the outcasts?

This question is no more relevant than on Easter, when our churches try especially to look their finest. When we assemble for worship this weekend, no one will set up tables to exchange currency. No one will lead in their oxen in hopes of getting rich. No one will tote a cage of high-priced pigeons. But our decorations may be elaborate. Our attire may be elegant. Our music may be world-class. We may put exuberant energy into these things, and make it an impressive spectacle. But if Jesus were to come, if he were to step into our churches this Sunday, he'd be looking for the rabble. Where are the misfits, the socially marginalized, the outcasts?

There is plenty of life in the veins of Easter to propel us beyond our comforts, our cliques, and our Sunday best, and send us powerfully out in the pursuit of the least.

HOLY

TUES
DAY

THE ESCALATING CONFLICT

Andreas Köstenberger & Justin Taylor

It is now Tuesday morning, March 31, A.D. 33. The disciples point to the withered fig tree that Jesus had cursed the day before. Jesus gives his disciples a simple lesson from it: Have faith in God. In particular, he says, if they have undoubting faith they can throw even the mountains into the sea.

Now if the disciples had ears to hear they would recognize that Jesus is talking about more than seemingly magical powers that can curse trees and crumble mountains. He is talking about realities bigger than this.

Note that he closes this mini-lesson on mountain-moving, undoubting faith by saying, "whenever you stand praying, *forgive*, if you have anything against anyone, so that your Father also who is in heaven may forgive you your trespasses" (Mark 11:25). Jesus is reminding them that failing to forgive looms as a bigger obstacle to answered prayer than a mountain. The disciples will soon face great challenges to their faith and their ability to forgive. Will they remember this withered tree on the road from Bethany?

As they approach the Holy City, the events from the day before could not have been far from their minds. As Jesus enters the Temple Mount, crowds gather to hear him teach (Luke 21:38), and the chief priests, scribes, and elders waste no time in making their move. They will try to lay four traps to ensnare their adversary.

Trap One: Whose Authority?

By whose authority, they demand to know, had Jesus carried out his actions the day before (Mark 11:28)? Jesus doesn't take the bait. Instead, he turns the tables on them with a question of his own: "Was the baptism of John from heaven or from man?" (Mark 11:30). If they respond "from heaven," the next question is obvious: Then why don't you believe the one about whom John testifies? If they retort "from man," they risk alienating the crowds that hold John in high esteem as a prophet.

Jesus then offers three parabolic stories (about two sons, murderous tenants, and guests at a wedding feast), all driving home the point that they are rejecting grace and truth in the service of hypocritical self-righteousness.

Trap Two: Whose Allegiance?

The leaders try a new tactic. They send Pharisees (a Jewish sect known for its zeal for the law) and Herodians (those loyal to Herod's dynasty) to ask him a question: "Is it lawful to pay taxes to Caesar, or not?" (Matt. 22:15–22; Mark 12:13–17; Luke 20:20–26). If he answers "yes," he shatters people's expectations of him as a Messiah who will overthrow Roman rule. If he says "no," he can be arrested for fomenting revolt.

But Jesus deftly evades the either-or dilemma: The

denarius has Caesar's image on it; as long as Caesar is in power, it is appropriate to pay taxes to him. And we are also to give God the things that are God's; since we are made in God's image, we owe everything—all that we have and all that we are—to him. Pay your taxes and worship God.

Trap Three: Whose Wife in the Resurrection?

After Jesus has silenced the Pharisees and Herodians, the Sadducees (a Jewish sect denying the end-time resurrection of the dead) try to ridicule Jesus's belief in the resurrection by asking a trick question about marriage in heaven (Matt. 22:23–33; Mark 12:18–27; Luke 20:27–40). Jesus tells them they do not understand the Scriptures (there is no marriage in heaven) or the power of God (God's self-affirmation in Ex. 3:6, 15–16 shows that he is a God of the living, not the dead). Like the others, their smirk turns to marvel as they grow silent.

Trap Four: Which Commandment?

Now the Pharisees send forth an expert in the law to question Jesus: Which of God's commands is the greatest (Matt. 22:34–40; Mark 12:28–34)? Jesus summarizes his answer in a word: *love* (to God and for neighbor: Deut. 6:4–5; Lev. 19:18). But Jesus discerns something different from this questioner, so he commends and implicitly invites him: "You are not far from the kingdom of God" (Mark 12:34).

Now it's Jesus's turn to initiate some questions with those who are trying to trap him. When he asks them a question about Psalm 110:1 and how the Messiah can be David's Lord, "no one was able to answer him a word, nor from that day did anyone dare to ask him any more questions" (Matt. 22:46). Jesus then launches a lengthy, scathing critique of the scribes and Pharisees, pronouncing seven woes of judgment upon these "hypocrites" and "blind guides" (Matt. 23:1–39; Mark 12:38–40; Luke 20:45–47).

This full-scale verbal assault removes all doubt concerning Jesus's intentions, agenda, and aims. He has no desire to ally himself with the current leadership. He has come to overthrow their authority. There's no way both sides can survive the escalating conflict. Either Jesus will assume power, or he must die.

Grace and Truth in Every Trap

With another tension-filled day behind them, Jesus and the disciples begin to head back to Bethany. They stop on the Mount of Olives to rest, giving them a wonderful view of Jerusalem as the sun begins to set behind it in the west. The disciples marvel at the size and the grandeur of these impressive buildings, but Jesus tells them that a day is soon coming when not a single stone will be left upon another. He goes on to explain that his followers will experience increasing persecution and tribulation, leading up to the final Day of Judgment. But their task is to remain vigilant and persist in faith.

Tuesday is now done. But Friday is coming. This is not the flannel-board Jesus some of us learned as children. This is the real, historical Jesus: fully in control as he responds with grace and truth to traps on all sides. He knows what he is doing. And he knows what is coming. Every word and every step is for the fame of his Father's name and the salvation of those willing to pick up their cross and die with him.

THE KING WE NEEDED, BUT NEVER WANTED

Marshall Segal

"The Son of Man will be delivered over to the chief priests and the scribes, and they will condemn him to death and deliver him over to the Gentiles." (Mark 10:33)

The road to Calvary was a road of confusion, not confidence, for those first disciples.

Three times Jesus explained to these men what it meant for him to be the Messiah. It was a horrific, yet hope-filled story: the murder of the promised king and then an inexplicable, unprecedented resurrection. It was way over the shortsighted, glory-hungry heads of Peter, James, John, and the others.

Their ignorance and wrong responses highlight ungodly grooves in the human heart. Their errors weren't peculiar to first-century fishermen. No, they're as pervasive and offensive in the church today. As we look forward to the horrors of Good Friday and the victory of Easter, we have to ask again, *Who do we say this Jesus is?* (Mark 8:29). Is he the Christ (on God's terms)? Or is he just the all-wise, all-powerful key to something or someone else?

The Son of Suffering, Not Comfort

The drama begins with that question, "Who do you say that I am?" "You are the Christ" (Mark 8:29). Peter was simultaneously very right, and very wrong. The word *Christ* was fitting in every respect. *It was the right answer.* But even though Peter's profile of the promised one was rightly named, it fell woefully flat.

Jesus paints a more detailed portrait of the Christ—the job description of the most important human who's ever lived:

> *He began to teach them that the Son of Man must suffer many things and be rejected by the elders and the chief priests and the scribes and be killed, and after three days rise again. (Mark 8:31)*

Peter (and presumably the other disciples) despised the idea of a suffering Christ. That's why he immediately gets in Jesus's face (Mark 8:32). Having rightly identified the Christ, he then presumed to have the perspective and authority to correct him. *Right*, yet tragically wrong.

The only Savior who truly saves, *only* saves through suffering. The cross was the only means of making us sinners right before a holy God. Our salvation was purchased with suffering, and it will be sealed and preserved with suffering (James 1:2–4), not comfort. We are promised comfort in the Christian life (2 Cor. 1:4), but not the cheap, temporal imitation we've grown accustomed to in our modern world.

If we come to the crucified one expecting him to make life easier and more comfortable, we're not listening to him. Jesus says, "If anyone would come after me, let him deny himself and take up his cross and follow me" (Mark 8:34).

The Son of Death, Then Life

Again, Jesus tells them the story of Calvary before it happens:

> *They went on from there and passed through Galilee. And he did not want anyone to know, for he was teaching his disciples, saying to them, "The Son of Man is going to be delivered into the hands of men, and they will kill him. And when he is killed, after three days he will rise." (Mark 9:30–31)*

Many of Jesus's followers thought Jesus came to rescue and reign now. They anticipated a physical and political freedom from the oppressive Roman rule. For them, the Christ was the key to their immediate, this-world issues. Life *now*. Freedom *now*. Power *now*. But Jesus, walking to the cross, instead says to wait. Be patient.

The rewards of following me, of finding life *in me* won't come in full today, but they will far surpass anything else you could have hoped for. In this story of life and hope and freedom, death comes first, and *then* life. Darkness, and *then* liberating, untouchable, unsearchable light.

The Son of Rejection, Not Approval

A third time, Jesus prepares them (and us) for his death:

> *Taking the twelve again, he began to tell them what*
> *was to happen to him, saying, "See, we are going up*
> *to Jerusalem, and the Son of Man will be delivered*
> *over to the chief priests and the scribes, and they will*
> *condemn him to death and deliver him over to the*
> *Gentiles. And they will mock him and spit on him,*
> *and flog him and kill him. And after three days he*
> *will rise." (Mark 10:32–34)*

The disciples certainly imagined there would be opposition in Jerusalem, but not like this. They expected a hostile takeover—and that did happen—but they expected Rome would be the bruised one, not the King. They were happy to have an opposed King, but not a rejected one, certainly not one who was betrayed, tortured, and executed.

Jesus did not come to purchase the approval of others. No, he "was despised and rejected by men; a man of sorrows, and acquainted with grief; and as one from whom men hide their faces he was despised" (Isa. 53:3). Why? Because it is God's approval we desperately need. And God's approval doesn't come by popular opinion, but by divine intervention—the substitution of his own Son in our place. We were saved through rejection (Isa. 53:3), and by God's grace, we will be carried and delivered through rejection (Matt. 10:22).

The call to Calvary—to follow Jesus—is a call to *die*, and rise again. It's a call to everlasting next-life gain through temporary this-life loss. Salvation isn't about securing our unique and selfish desires and ambitions on this earth, but about securing and preparing our souls for another world, a new creation built and preserved for our glory in God's and our satisfaction in him.

To truly live, we must surrender to the King we really needed, not the one we might have imagined for ourselves.

SPY
WEDN

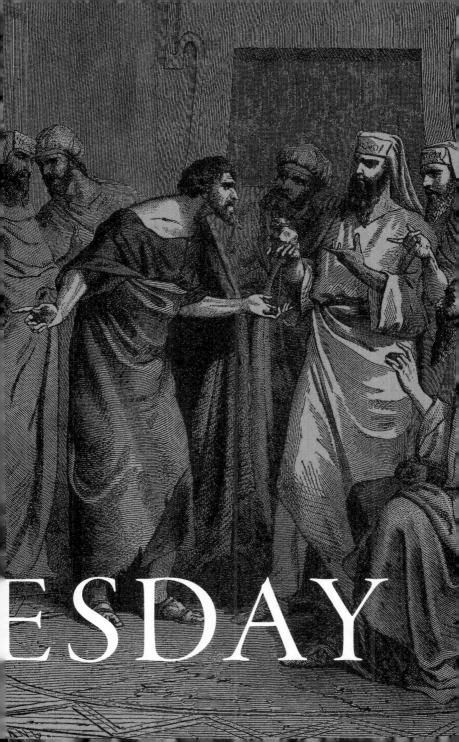

ESDAY

BETRAYED BY ONE OF HIS OWN

David Mathis

Wednesday went quietly. Too quietly.

With the previous three days awash in drama—Sunday's triumphal entry, Monday's temple cleansing, and Tuesday's temple controversies—now Wednesday, April 1, A.D. 33, comes like the calm before the storm.

But out of sight, lurking in the shadows, evil is afoot. The church has long called it "Spy Wednesday," as the dark conspiracy against Jesus races forward, not just from enemies outside, but now with a traitor from within. It is this day when the key pieces come together in the plot for the greatest sin in all of history: the murder of the Son of God.

The Plot Thickens

Jesus wakes again just outside Jerusalem, in Bethany, where he has been staying at the home of Mary, Martha, and Lazarus. His teaching again attracts a crowd in the temple. But now the Jewish leaders, silenced by Jesus the day before, will leave him be. Today they will avoid public confrontation and instead connive in private.

Caiaphas, the high priest, gathers to his private residence the chief priests and Pharisees—two competing groups, typically at odds, now bedfellows in their ache to be rid of the Galilean. They scheme to kill him, but don't have all the pieces in place yet. They fear the approving masses, and don't want to stir up the assembled hordes during Passover. The initial plan is to wait till after the feast, unless some unforeseen opportunity emerges.

Enter the traitor.

The Miser and His Money

The Gospel accounts point to the same precipitating event: the anointing at Bethany.

Jesus was approached by a woman—we learn from John 12:3 that it was Mary, the sister of Martha. She took "very expensive ointment" and anointed Jesus. An objection comes from the disciples—John 12:4 says it was Judas—"Why was this ointment not sold for three hundred denarii and given to the poor?" This was, after all, "a very large sum," more than a year's wages for a soldier or common laborer. It would have been enough money to finance a family for more than a year, and could have gone a long way for charity.

But Jesus doesn't share Judas's miserliness. Here he finds extravagance in its rightful place. The kingdom he brings resists mere utilitarian economics. He sees in Mary's "waste" a worshiping impulse that goes beyond the rational, calculated, efficient use of time and money. For Mary, Jesus is worth every shekel and more. The Anointed himself says what she has done is "a beautiful thing" (Matt. 26:10).

Judas, on the other hand, is not so convinced. And contrary to appearances, the miser's protest betrays a heart of greed. Judas's concern comes "not because he cared about the poor, but because he was a thief, and having charge of the moneybag he used to help himself to what was put into it" (John 12:6). The traitor had long been on a trajectory of sin and hard-heartedness, but the last straw is this extravagant anointing.

Satan finds a foothold in this heart in love with money, and what wickedness follows. Incensed about this "waste" of a year's wages, he goes to the chief priests and becomes just the window of opportunity the conspirators are looking for. The spy will lead them to Jesus at the opportune time when the crowds have dispersed. And the greedy miser will do it for only thirty pieces of silver, which Exodus 21:32 establishes as the price of the life of a slave.

Why the Insult of Betrayal?

Why would God have it go down like this? If Jesus truly is being "delivered up according to the definite plan and foreknowledge of God" (Acts 2:23), and his enemies are doing just as God's hand and plan "had predestined to take place" (Acts 4:28), why design it like this, with one of his own disciples betraying him? Why add the insult of betrayal to the injury of the cross?

We find a clue when Jesus quotes Psalm 41:9 in forecasting Judas's defection: "He who ate my bread has lifted his heel against me" (John 13:18). King David knew the pain not just of being conspired against by his enemies, but betrayed by his friend. So now the Son of David walks the same path in his agony. Here Judas turns on him. Soon Peter will deny him, and then the remaining ten will scatter.

From the beginning of his public ministry, the disciples have been at his side. They have learned from him, traveled with him, ministered with him, been his earthly companions, and comforted him as he walked this otherwise lonely road to Jerusalem.

But now, as Jesus's hour comes, this burden he must bear alone. The definitive work will be no team effort. The Anointed must go forward unaccompanied, as even his friends betray him, deny him, and disperse. As Donald Macleod observes, "Had the redemption of the world depended on the diligence of the disciples (or even their staying awake) it would never have been accomplished."[1]

As he lifts "loud cries and tears" (Heb. 5:7) in the garden, the heartbreak of David is added to his near emotional breakdown: "Even my close friend in whom I trusted, who ate my bread, has lifted his heel against me" (Ps. 41:9). He is forsaken by his closest earthly associates, one of them even becoming a spy against him. But even this is not the bottom of his anguish. The depth comes in the cry of dereliction, "My God! My God! Why have you forsaken me?" (Matt. 27:46).

But more remarkable than this depth of forsakenness is the height of love he will show. Greater love has no one than this, that he lay down his life for his friends, even when they have forsaken him.

---

1 Donald Macleod, *The Person of Christ* (Downers Grove: IVP Academic, 1998), 173.

MUTINY AGAINST THE MESSIAH

Johnathon Bowers

Judas Iscariot, who was one of the twelve, went to the chief priests in order to betray him to them. (Mark 14:10)

The chief priests wanted him dead. But they couldn't kill him in the open. No, the people liked him too much. And their public image was fragile enough as it was. Jesus had seen to that. The temple-cleansing. The parables. The shrewd evasion of every verbal trap they could drum up. They needed a way to pounce on him in private. And it had to be quick.

He was in Jerusalem, so the time was ripe. But Passover was in two days. *Two days.* What would they do?

At this point in Mark 14, we leave the chief priests to their bloodlust and hand-wringing and shift our attention to a house in Bethany, just a couple miles east of Jerusalem. Simon the leper was hosting a meal. Jesus, the disciples, and some others were reclining around the dinner table. And then *she* came. John 12:3 tells us that the woman was Mary the sister of Lazarus, but Mark is content to leave her nameless: "A woman came with an alabaster flask of ointment of pure nard, very costly, and she broke the flask and poured it over his head" (Mark 14:3).

Very costly. In fact, for some at the table, it was too costly.

Traitor among the Twelve

A year's worth of wages fell out of the flask. And for some of the guests, the fragrance that filled the room became the stench of lost opportunity. "Why was the ointment wasted like that?" they complained. "For this ointment could have been sold for more than three hundred denarii and given to the poor" (Mark 14:4–5). Stuff and nonsense. They didn't care about the poor. What they really wanted was a bloated pouch of coins in the benevolence budget. At least, that's what Judas wanted. Selling the ointment would give him a fresh stash of funds from which to filch (John 12:6).

Jesus rebuked the murmuring, much like he had the Sea of Galilee. But mutiny was afoot. Mark shifts his narrative focus from Bethany back to the chief priests. Judas, the spy, winded from the two-mile hike back to Jerusalem, found the religious leaders in their lair. Maybe he was seething from the shame he had received back at Simon's house. Maybe his love for money had so muddied his thinking that he couldn't get over the waste he had just seen. And not just waste, but waste that Jesus *applauded*. "She has done a beautiful thing to me," Jesus said. "She has anointed my body beforehand for burial" (Mark 14:6, 8).

Maybe Judas was stewing over these words as he huffed his way over to the Holy City. *All right, Jesus. You're ready for burial? I'll make sure you get one. After all, I'd hate to see all that ointment go to waste.*

Thirty Pieces of Silver

And so, Judas offered the chief priests the solution they had been waiting for: He would betray his master. But not without something in return. Mark simply records that the chief priests promised to give Judas money (Mark 14:11). The word "promise" suggests that Judas wasn't surprised by the offer. It appears that he had pressed the priests for payment. Matthew tells us as much, in fact: "Then one of the twelve, whose name was Judas Iscariot, went to the chief priests and said, 'What will you give me if I deliver him over to you?' And they paid him thirty pieces of silver" (Matt. 26:14–15).

The drama of Mark 14 revolves around two characters—the woman and Judas—and their opposing reactions to Jesus. But there is a third character, an antagonist both sinister and stealthy.

Money.

Notice how quickly Judas and his fellow grumblers are able to appraise the value of the ointment at Simon's house. Like veteran pawnbrokers, they could intuit at a glance how much something was worth. The nard had barely left the flask before they were calculating, "This ointment could have been sold for more than three hundred denarii" (Mark 14:5).

Blind to the Value of Christ

And yet, the irony of Mark 14 is that Judas could see the value of the ointment rolling down Jesus's head, but he couldn't see the value of Jesus. He was a pawnbroker with cataracts. That's why he took such offense at the woman. The woman, on the other hand, could see both the value of the ointment *and* the value of Jesus. That's why she broke the flask.

Spy Wednesday is a tragic reminder of 1 Tim. 6:10: "The love of money is a root of all kinds of evils. It is through this craving that some have wandered away from the faith and pierced themselves with many pangs."

But Spy Wednesday is also full of hope, because it shows us that the beauty of Jesus can break the spell of financial gain. This is the woman's message to us, a message that Jesus wanted us to hear again and again: "Truly, I say to you, wherever the gospel is proclaimed in the whole world, what she has done will be told in memory of her" (Mark 14:9).

MAU

THURS
DAY
NDY

MORNING

THE GREATEST PRAYER
IN THE WORLD

John Piper

It is Thursday, the night before Jesus's crucifixion. This evening has been laden with teaching (John 13–17), shocking with foot-washing by the greatest for the least (John 13:3–20), epoch-making with the institution of the Lord's Supper (Matt. 26:20–30; Mark 14:17–26; Luke 22:14–20), and pivotal with the departure of Judas (John 13:30).

Now Jesus and the eleven have gone to the Garden of Gethsemane (John 18:1; Mark 14:32). Here Jesus prays the greatest prayer in the world. What hung in the balance was the glory of God's grace and the salvation of the world. The success of Jesus's mission to earth depended on Jesus's prayer and the answer given. He prayed with reverence and his request was given.

The question I would like to try to answer is: How does Hebrews 5:7 relate to the prayers in Gethsemane? Hebrews 5:7 says, "In the days of his flesh, Jesus offered up prayers and supplications, with loud cries and tears, to him who was able to save him from death, and he was heard because of his reverence." He was heard. He got his request. What does this refer to in Jesus's life?

Loud Cries in the Garden

Nothing in Jesus's experience comes closer to this description than the prayers of Gethsemane. "Jesus offered up prayers and supplications, with loud cries and tears," corresponds emotionally to Luke 22:44, "Being in agony he prayed more earnestly; and his sweat became like great drops of blood falling down to the ground." "Loud cries and tears" is a description of the "agony" of Jesus.

What was the content of Jesus's "prayers and supplications" in Hebrews 5:7? If we assume the content was: "Remove this cup from me" (Mark 14:36), then what would it mean that "he was heard because of his reverence" (Heb. 5:7)? Hebrews teaches that, precisely because of his "godly fear," Jesus "was heard," that is, he received his request.

But the cup was not removed. He suffered the fullness of physical pain and divine wrath. So in what sense was Jesus "heard because of his reverence"?

His First Prayer and the Angel's Help

Both Matthew and Mark portray Jesus as praying three separate times, and each time returning to the sleeping Peter, James, and John. Luke, on the other hand, gives a single summary description of Jesus's prayers, and includes a detail that points to an answer to our question, namely, the visitation of the angel. Luke writes,

*He withdrew from them about a stone's throw, and
knelt down and prayed, saying, "Father, if you are
willing, remove this cup from me. Nevertheless, not
my will, but yours, be done." And there appeared to
him an angel from heaven, strengthening him. And
being in an agony he prayed more earnestly; and his
sweat became like great drops of blood falling down
to the ground. (Luke 22:41–44)*

Before the angel came "to strengthen" him, Jesus prayed
that the cup be removed (Luke 22:42). Then the angel came,
"strengthening him." Strengthening him for what? Presumably to do what he had to do. In other words, the angel was
God's response to Jesus's first prayer. The angel bears God's
message that there is no other way, but I will help you. Do
not turn from your mission now, in spite of the terrifying
prospect. I will help you. Here is my angel to strengthen you.

Then the question is: What was the content of the
prayers that followed? Luke 22:44 says, "And being in an
agony he prayed more earnestly." Does this mean he kept
on saying: "Remove this cup from me," even more earnestly? That assumption would be unworthy of Jesus. What
then was he praying? And is this different prayer what
Hebrews says "was heard because of his reverence"?

He Prays a Second Time

According to Matthew, when Jesus went away a second time
to pray, he did not say the identical words as the first time.
The first time he said, "My Father, if it be possible, let this cup
pass from me." The second time he said, "My Father, if this
cannot pass unless I drink it, your will be done" (Matt. 26:42).

May we not assume that the angel had come to Jesus the first time he prayed, and had made plain to Jesus that it was, in fact, not possible for the cup to pass from him, but that God would help him drink it? Which is why, in his second prayer, Jesus does not ask for the cup to be removed, but instead asks for God's will to be done in view of the revealed fact that "the cup cannot pass": "If *this cannot pass unless I drink it* [which has now been made plain to me by the coming of the angel], your will be done."

When Mark says, of the second prayer of Jesus, "And again he went away and prayed, *saying the same words*" (Mark 14:39), it need not contradict this, as though *only* the same words were spoken all three times. "The same words" may simply refer to, "Your will be done," which indeed Jesus prays each time.

If we are on the right track, then the content of Jesus's supplications after the angel came was not the same as before. He did not go on praying: "Let this cup pass from me." It says, "And being in an agony he prayed more earnestly" (Luke 22:44). If he was not praying more earnestly for the cup to be removed, then what was he praying?

His Greatest Act of Obedience

Hebrews 5:7 says, "Jesus offered up prayers and supplications, with loud cries and tears, *to him who was able to save him from death*, and he was heard because of his reverence." If "save his soul from death" does not mean, "Remove this cup from me," what does it mean? For he was certainly

---

2 Jonathan Edwards, "Christ's Agony," sermon available online at http://www.ccel.org/ccel/edwards/sermons.agony.html.

heard and received this request.

Jonathan Edwards answers,

> *This was the greatest act of obedience that Christ was to perform. He prays for strength and help, that his poor feeble human nature might be supported, that he might not fail in this great trial, that he might not sink and be swallowed up, and his strength so overcome that he should not hold out, and finish the appointed obedience.*
>
> *He was afraid lest his poor feeble strength should be overcome, and that he should fail in so great a trial, that he should be swallowed up by that death that he was to die, and so should not be saved from death; and therefore he offered up strong crying and tears unto him that was able to strengthen him, and support, and save him from death, that the death he was to suffer might not overcome his love and obedience, but that he might overcome death, and so be saved from it.*[2]

Jesus did not go on praying for the cup to pass. He went on praying for success in drinking it.

When Paul says, of Jesus's resurrection, "*Therefore*, God has highly exalted him" (Phil. 2:9), the "therefore" refers to Jesus's unwavering obedience unto death: "Being found in human form, he humbled himself by becoming obedient to the point of death, even death on a cross. Therefore..." (Phil. 2:8). God saved Jesus from death because he was obedient. His prayers were answered.

The Father's Answer

If Jesus had not been obedient unto death, he would have

been swallowed up by death forever and there would be no resurrection, no salvation, and no future world filled with the glory of God's grace and God's children. This is what Jesus prayed for "to him who was able to save him from death"—that is, save him from a death that would not succeed its saving mission.

"He was heard for his godly fear." God did save him from the threat that such a death posed to his obedience. Jesus did succeed. There is salvation for all who believe. There will be a new world full of the glory of God's grace and God's children.

And all of this is owing to the greatest prayer in the world. Every hope of the gospel succeeds because of Jesus's reverent earnestness in prayer, and the answer of the Father. "Being in an agony he prayed more earnestly... and he was heard because of his reverence" (Luke 22:44; Heb. 5:7).

Evidently, by the time Jesus was done praying in Gethsemane, the Father had not only made clear that there is no other way than the cross, but also that this way would succeed. The Lamb would have the reward of his suffering. He will "see his offspring; he will prolong his days; the will of the Lord will prosper in his hand. Out of the anguish of his soul he will see and be satisfied" (Isa. 53:10–11).

Surely this is why Hebrews 12:2 could say, "For the joy that was set before him he endured the cross." Beneath the terrors of present agony was the taste of future joy. The angel had come, "strengthening him"—clarifying, confirming, connecting the coming joy.

NOT MY WILL BE DONE

Jon Bloom

"Father, all things are possible for you. Remove this
cup from me. Yet not what I will, but what you will."
(Mark 14:36)

Darkness had descended on Jerusalem. Its residents had finished their Passover meals. The lamb and unleavened bread had been consumed; the sandals, staffs, and belts put away (Ex. 12:1–11).

In Caiaphas's house, a conference was underway with some members of the Sanhedrin, some officers of the temple guard, and one of Jesus's closest friends. In the secluded hillside olive garden of Gethsemane, just outside the city's eastern wall opposite the temple, Jesus sat with his other eleven closest friends. The eleven friends could not stay awake. Jesus could not sleep.

The Great Passover Unveiled

Earlier that evening, Jesus had shared with his disciples the most marvelous Passover meal of all time, though his disciples only recognized this in retrospect. Jesus had "earnestly desired" to eat it with them (Luke 22:15). For the Great Passover, the one for which the Passover in Egypt was a type and shadow, was about to take place.

The angel of death was coming to claim the Firstborn Son (Col. 1:15). The worst plague of God's judgment was about to fall. But this Firstborn Son, being all and in all (Col. 3:11), was also the Passover Lamb who would be slain to take away the sins of the world (John 1:29; Rev. 5:6). The eternally obedient Firstborn Son, the spotless Lamb of God, would take on himself all the sin of the sons and daughters of disobedience (Eph. 5:6), his blood would cover them, they would receive his righteousness (2 Cor. 5:21), and they would forever be shielded from the death angel's blow (John 11:26).

So the Firstborn of many brothers (Rom. 8:29), the Great Passover Lamb, had taken bread and wine and said to the first eleven of those brothers, "This is my body... This is my blood..." (Mark 14:22–25). And in doing so, the old Passover was subsumed into the new Passover.

From that moment on, the new Passover meal would be eaten in remembrance of Jesus (1 Cor. 11:23–26) and how he delivered all his brothers and sisters out of the slavery of sin and death and led them into the promised eternal kingdom of the beloved Son (Col. 1:13).

Nine Unfathomable Words

But now, among the olive trees, Jesus was praying. Many

times he had prayed in "desolate places" (Luke 5:16). Yet never had he known desolation like this.

In this familiar garden of prayer, Jesus looked deeply into the Father's Cup he was about to drink and was terrified. Everything in his human flesh wanted to flee the impending physical torture of crucifixion. And his Holy Spirit groaned with ineffable dread at the far greater impending spiritual torture of being forsaken by his Father.

Such was his distress over this "baptism" (Luke 12:50), the very thing he had come into the world to accomplish (John 12:27), that Jesus cried out, "Father, all things are possible for you. Remove this cup from me. Yet not what I will, but what you will" (Mark 14:36).

Yet not what I will, but what you will. Nine words. Nine unfathomable words.

God, having longed, and even pled, to be delivered from God's will, expressed in these nine simple words a humble faith in and submission to God's will that was more beautiful than all the glory in the created heavens and earth combined. Mystery upon Trinitarian mystery: God did not consider equality with God a thing to be grasped, but became obedient to God's will, even if it meant God dying an incomprehensibly horrifying death on a Roman cross (Phil. 2:6, 8). God wanted God's will to be done on earth as it is in heaven, even though in that dark moment, God wished in body and soul that God's will could be done another way.

Obedience in Suffering

And in that moment, another mystery came into view. God the Son, perfectly obedient to God the Father from all eternity, "learned obedience through what he suffered" (Heb. 5:8). Never has another human felt such an intense desire to be spared the will of God. And never has any human exercised such humble, obedient faith in the Father's will. "And being made perfect"—having exercised perfectly obedient trust in his Father in all possible dimensions—"he became the source of eternal salvation to all who obey him" (Heb. 5:9).

As the Son learned this perfect and preeminently humble obedience as he yielded to the Father's will, the first drops of his bloody agony seeped out of his pores (Luke 22:44).

Barely a kilometer away, in the high priest's courtyard, his treacherous disciple prepared to lead a small, torch-bearing contingent of soldiers and servants to a familiar garden of prayer.

Your Will Be Done

No one understands better than God how difficult it can be for a human to embrace the will of God. And no human has suffered more in embracing the will of God the Father than God the Son. When Jesus calls us to follow him, whatever the cost, he is not calling us to do something he is either unwilling to do or has never done himself.

That is why we look to Jesus as the "author and perfecter of our faith" (Heb. 12:2). He is our great high priest who understands, far better than we do, what it's like to willingly and faithfully endure the sometimes excruciating, momentarily painful will of God for the sake of the eternal joy set before us (Heb. 4:15; 12:2). And now he always lives to intercede for us so that we will make it through the pain to the eternal joy (Heb. 7:25).

So this Maundy Thursday, we join God the Son in praying to God the Father, "Your will be done" (Matt. 6:10). And if we find that, in body and soul, we wish God's will for us could be done in a way different from what God's will appears to be, we may wholeheartedly pray with Jesus, "Father, all things are possible for you. Remove this cup from me." But only if we will also pray with Jesus these nine gloriously humble words, "Yet not what I will, but what you will."

Because God's will for us, however painful now, will result in joy inexpressible and full of glory, and the salvation of our souls (1 Pet. 1:8–9).

GOOD

FRIDAY

IT IS FINISHED

Jon Bloom

It is Friday, April 3, A.D. 33. It is the darkest day in human history, though most humans have no clue of this. In Rome, Tiberius attends to the demanding business of the empire. Throughout the inhabited world, babies are born, people eat and drink, marry and are given in marriage, barter in marketplaces, sail merchant ships, and fight battles. Children play, old women gossip, young men lust, and people die.

But today, one death, one brutal, gruesome death, the worst and best of all human deaths, will leave upon the canvas of human history the darkest brushstroke. In Jerusalem, God the Son, the Creator of all that is (John 1:3), will be executed.

The Garden

The Jewish day dawns with night, and never has it been more fitting, since today the hour has come and the power of darkness (Luke 22:53). Jesus is in Gethsemane, where he has prayed with loud cries and tears, being heard by his Father (Heb. 5:7) whose will will be done. Jesus hears noises and looks up. Torches and hushed voices signal the arrest party's arrival.

Jesus wakes his sleepy friends who are jarred alert at the sight of their brother, Judas, betraying his Rabbi with a kiss. Soldiers and servants encircle Jesus. Peter, flushed with anger, pulls out his sword and lunges at those nearest Jesus. Malchus flinches, but not enough. Blinding pain and blood surge where his ear had been. Voices speak, but Malchus only hears the screaming wound, which he's grabbed with both hands. He feels a hand touch his hands and the pain vanishes. Under his hands is an ear. Stunned, he looks at Jesus, already being led away. Disciples are scattering. Malchus looks down at his bloody hands.

The Sanhedrin

Jesus is led brusquely into the house of Annas, a former High Priest, who questions him about his teaching. Jesus knows this informal interrogation is meant to catch him disoriented and unguarded. He is neither, and gives this manipulative leader nothing. Rather, he refers Annas to his hearers and is struck with irony by a Jewish officer for showing disrespect. Frustrated, Annas sends Jesus on to his son-in-law Caiaphas, the current High Priest.

At Caiaphas's house the trial gets underway quickly. Morning will come fast. The Council needs a damning verdict by daybreak. The examination proceeds as bleary-eyed Sanhedrin members continue to file in.

The trial has been assembled hastily and witnesses haven't been screened well. Testimonies don't line up.

Council members look disconcerted. Jesus is silent as a lamb. Irritated and impatient, Caiaphas cuts to the quick: "I adjure you by the living God, tell us if you are the Christ, the Son of God" (Matt. 26:63).

The hour has come. Charged in the name of his Father to answer, Jesus speaks the words that seal the doom for which he had come to endure (John 12:27): "You have said so. But I tell you, from now on you will see the Son of Man seated at the right hand of Power and coming on the clouds of heaven" (Matt. 26:64).

In a moment of law-breaking (Lev. 21:10) politically religious theater, Caiaphas tears his robes in feigned outrage and thinly concealed relief over Jesus's blasphemy. He declares the trial's end with, "What further testimony do we need? We have heard it ourselves from his own lips" (Luke 22:71).

As the sun breaks over Jerusalem's eastern ridge, Judas swings from his own belt, Peter writhes in the grief of his failure, and Jesus's face is streaked with dried blood and saliva from the pre-dawn sport of the temple police. The Council's verdict: guilty of blasphemy. Their sentence: death. But it's a sentence they cannot carry out. Rome refuses to delegate capital punishment.

The Governor

Pilate's mood, already sour over the Sanhedrin's sudden insistent intrusion so early in the morning, worsens as he grasps the situation. They want him to execute a Galilean "prophet." His seasoned instincts tell him something isn't right. He questions Jesus and then tells the Council, "I find no guilt in this man" (Luke 23:4).

A game of political chess ensues between Pilate and the Sanhedrin, neither realizing that they are pawns, not kings.

Pilate makes a move. As a Galilean, Jesus falls under Herod Antipas's jurisdiction. Let Herod judge. Herod initially receives Jesus happily, hoping to see a miracle. But Jesus refuses to entertain or even respond. Antipas, disappointed, blocks the move by returning Jesus to Pilate.

Pilate makes another move. He offers to release Jesus as this year's annual Passover-pardoned prisoner. The Council blocks the move. "Not this man, but Barabbas!" they cry (John 18:40). Pilate is astounded. The Sanhedrin prefers a thief and murderer to this peasant prophet?

Pilate tries another move. He has Jesus severely flogged and humiliated, hoping to curb the Council's blood thirst. Again the move is blocked when the Council insists that Jesus must be crucified because "he has made himself the Son of God" (John 19:7). Check. Pilate's fear grows. Jesus's divine claim could threaten Rome. Worse, it could be true. Roman deities supposedly could take on human form. His further questioning of Jesus unnerves him.

One last move. Pilate tries to persuade the Sanhedrin to release Jesus. One last block and trap. "If you release this man, you are not Caesar's friend. Everyone who makes himself a king opposes Caesar" (John 19:12). The Council has Pilate where they want him: cornered. Checkmate.

And the triune God has the Council, Pilate, and Satan where he wants them. They would have no authority over the Son at all unless it had been given them from above (John 19:11). Fallen Jews, Gentiles, and spiritual powers unwittingly collaborate in executing the only innocent death that could possibly grant the guilty life. Checkmate.

The Cross

Morning wanes as Jesus stumbles out of the Praetorium, horribly beaten and bleeding profusely. The Roman soldiers had been brutal in their creative cruelty. Thorns have ripped Jesus's scalp, and his back is one grotesque, oozing wound. Golgotha is barely a third of a mile through the Garden Gate, but Jesus has no strength to manage the forty-pound crossbar. Simon of Cyrene is drafted from the crowd.

Twenty-five minutes later, Jesus is hanging in sheer agony on one of the cruelest instruments of torture ever devised. Nails have been driven through his wrists (which we only know about because of the doubt Thomas will express in a couple days—see John 20:25). A sign above Jesus declares in Greek, Latin, and Aramaic who he is: the King of the Jews.

The King is flanked on either side by thieves and around him are gawkers and mockers. "Let him save himself, if he is the Christ of God, his Chosen One!" some yell (Luke 23:35). One dying thief even joins in the derision. They do not understand that if the King saves himself, their only hope for salvation is lost. Jesus asks his Father to forgive them. The other crucified thief sees a Messiah in the mutilated man beside him, and he asks the Messiah to remember him. Jesus's prayer is beginning to be answered. Hundreds of millions will follow.

It is mid-afternoon now and the eerie darkness that has fallen has everyone on edge. But for Jesus, the darkness is a horror he has never known. This, more than the nails and thorns and lashings, is what made him sweat blood in the garden. The Father's wrath is hitting him in full force. He is in that moment no longer the Blessed, but the

Cursed (Gal. 3:13). He has become sin (2 Cor. 5:21). In terrifying isolation, cut off from his Father and all humans, he screams, "*Eli, Eli, lema sabachthani,*" Aramaic for "My God, my God, why have you forsaken me?" (Matt. 27:46; Ps. 22:1). No greater love (John 15:13), humility (Phil. 2:8), or obedience (Heb. 5:8) has ever or will ever be displayed.

Shortly after 3:00 P.M., Jesus whispers hoarsely for a drink. In love, he has drained the cup of his Father's wrath to the dregs. He has borne our full curse. There is no debt left to pay, and he has nothing left to give. The wine moistens his mouth just enough to say one final word: "It is finished" (John 19:30). And God the Son dies.

It is the worst and best of all human deaths. For on this tree he bears our sins in his body (1 Pet. 2:24), "the righteous for the unrighteous, that he might bring us to God" (1 Pet. 3:18). And now it is finished.

The Tomb

A bright irony on this darkest of days is that the men who step forward to claim the corpse of the Christ for burial are not family members or disciples. They are members of the Sanhedrin: Joseph of Arimathea and Nicodemus. It is one more unexpected thread of grace woven into this tapestry of redemption. They quickly wrap Jesus's body in a sheet and lay it in a nearby tomb. Evening is falling, and they don't have time to fully dress it with spices.

Mary Magdalene and Mary the mother of Joses accompany them, careful to note the tomb's location. They plan to return with more spices after the Sabbath, on the first day of the week, to make sure that it is finished.

WHY HAVE YOU FORSAKEN ME?

Donald Macleod

At the ninth hour Jesus cried out in a loud voice,
"Eloi, Eloi, lama sabachthani?" *(Mark 15:34)*

Up to this point, the narrative of the crucifixion has focused on the physical sufferings of Jesus: the flogging, the crown of thorns, and his immolation on the cross. Six hours have now passed since the nails were driven home. The crowds have jeered, darkness has covered the land, and now, suddenly, after a long silence, comes this anguished cry from the depths of the Savior's soul.

The words are an Aramaic-tinged quotation from Psalm 22, and although Matthew and Mark both offer a translation for the benefit of Gentile readers, they clearly want us to hear the exact words that Jesus spoke. At his lowest ebb, his mind instinctively breathes the Psalter, and from it he borrows the words that express the anguish, not now of his body, but of his soul.

He bore in his soul, wrote Calvin, "the terrible torments of a condemned and lost man."[3] But dare we, on such hallowed ground, seek more clarity?

Against All Hope

There are certainly some very clear negatives. The forsakenness cannot mean, for example, that the eternal communion between the Father, the Son, and the Holy Spirit was broken. God could not cease to be triune.

Neither could it mean that the Father ceased to love the Son: especially not here, and not now, when the Son was offering the greatest tribute of filial piety that the Father had ever received.

Nor again could it mean that the Holy Spirit had ceased to minister to the Son. He had come down upon him at his baptism not merely for one fleeting moment, but to remain on him (John 1:32), and he would be there to the last as the eternal Spirit through whom the Son offered himself to God (Heb. 9:14).

And finally, the words are not a cry of despair. Despair would have been sin. Even in the darkness God was, "*My God,*" and though there was no sign of him, and though the pain obscured the promises, somewhere in the depths of his soul there remained the assurance that God was holding him. What was true of Abraham was truer still of Jesus: Against all hope, he in hope believed (Rom. 4:18).

---

3 John Calvin, *Institutes of the Christian Religion.* 2 vols. Translated by F. L. Battles (Philadelphia: Westminster, 1960), II: xvi, 10.

Truly Forsaken

Yet, with all these qualifiers, this was a real forsaking. Jesus did not merely *feel* forsaken. He was forsaken; and not only by his disciples, but by God himself. It was the Father who had delivered him up to Judas, to the Jews, to Pilate, and finally to the cross itself.

And now, when he had cried, God had closed his ears. The crowd had not stopped jeering, the demons had not stopped taunting, the pain had not abated. Instead, every circumstance bespoke the anger of God; and there was no countering voice. This time, no word came from heaven to remind him that he was God's Son, and greatly loved. No dove came down to assure him of the Spirit's presence and ministry. No angel came to strengthen him. No redeemed sinner bowed to thank him.

Bearing the Curse

Who was he? He cries out in Aramaic, but he doesn't use the greatest of all the Aramaic words, *Abba*. Even in the anguish of Gethsemane, distraught and overborne though he was, he had been able to use it (Mark 14:36). But not here.

Like Abraham and Isaac going up to Mount Moriah, he and the Father had gone up to Calvary together. But now *Abba* is not there. Only *El* is there: God All-mighty, God All-holy. And he is before *El*, not now as his Beloved Son, but as the Sin of the World. That is his identity: the character in which he stands before Absolute Integrity.

It is not that he bears some vague relation to sinners. He is one of them, numbered with transgressors. Indeed, he is all of them. He is sin (2 Cor. 5:21), condemned to bear its curse; and he has no cover. None can serve as his advocate. Nothing can be offered as his expiation. He must bear all, and *El* will not, cannot, spare him till the ransom is paid in full. Will that point ever be reached? What if his mission fails?

The sufferings of his soul, as the old divines used to say, were the soul of his suffering, and into that soul we can see but dimly. Public though the cry was, it expressed the intensely private anguish of a tension between the sin-bearing Son and his heavenly Father: the whirlwind of sin at its most dreadful, God forsaken by God.

His Anguish of Soul

But no less challenging than the torment in Jesus's soul is his question, "Why?"

Is it the why of protest: the cry of the innocent against unjust suffering? The premise is certainly correct. He is innocent. But he has lived his whole life conscious that he is the sin-bearer and has to die as the redemption-price for the many. Has he forgotten that now?

Or is it the why of incomprehension, as if he doesn't understand why he's here? Has he forgotten the eternal covenant? Perhaps. His mind, as a human mind, could not be focused on all the facts at the same time, and for the moment the pain, the divine anger, and the fear of eternal perdition (the cross being God's last word) occupy all his thoughts.

Or is it the why of amazement, as he confronts a dreadfulness he could never have anticipated? He had known from the beginning that he would die a violent death (Mark 2:20), and in Gethsemane he had looked it in the eye, and shuddered. But now he is tasting it in all its bitterness, and the reality is infinitely worse than the prospect.

Never before had anything come between him and his Father, but now the sin of the whole world has come between them, and he is caught in this dreadful vortex of the curse. It is not that *Abba* is not there, but that he is there, as the Judge of all the earth who could condone nothing and could not spare even his own Son (Rom. 8:32).

The Cup Is Drained

Now, Jesus's mind is near the limits of its endurance. We, sitting in the gallery of history, are sure of the outcome. He, suffering in human nature the fury of hell, is not. He is standing where none has stood before or since, enduring at one tiny point in space and in one tiny moment of time, all that sin deserved: the curse in unmitigated concentration.

But then, suddenly, it is over. The sacrifice is complete, the curtain torn, and the way into the Holiest opened once and for all; and now Jesus's joy finds expression in the words of another psalm, Psalm 31:5. In the original, it had not contained the word *Abba*, but Jesus inserts it: "Father, into your hands I commit my spirit" (Luke 23:46).

We have no means of knowing what intervened between the two cries. We know only that the Cup is drained and the curse exhausted, and that the Father now proudly holds out his hands to the spirit of his Beloved Son.

HOLY

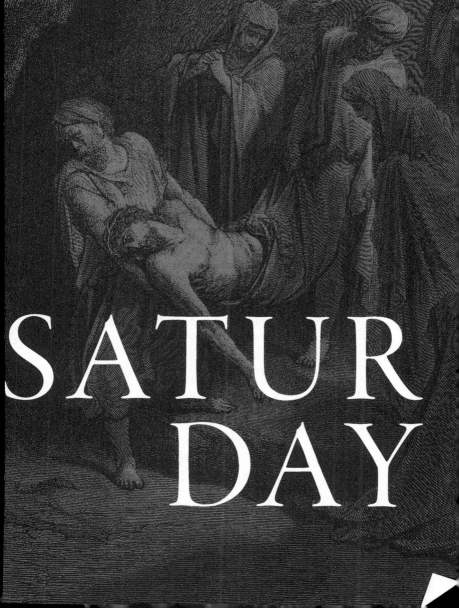

SATURDAY

LET HIS BLOOD BE ON US

Marshall Segal

Holy Week waits in relative silence on Saturday. The tomb has been sealed, the guards stand watch, the disciples likely hide in confusion, fear, and devastation. And the Savior lies lifeless, having surrendered all to save his people from their sins.

How would you process the horrors of the last couple of days in the quiet, disturbing shadow of the cross? The disciples had to have a thousand painful questions. How could he be the long-awaited King if he was just killed? Is there something we could have done to stop it? If they tortured and slaughtered him like that, what will they do to us? It was all playing back through their minds while they waited on Saturday.

We too still hear the dark, sobering echoes of Thursday and Friday. But we wait with expectation for tomorrow—for the empty grave and risen King. Filled with hope, we can look back into the crowd that crucified Jesus and see our old selves, and then forward, in preparation for Easter, rejoicing in the transformation that's taken place in us because of his sacrifice. We've been covered by the blood that confounded those first followers.

The Pro-Choice Pilate

One of the echoes sounds from Matthew 27. Jesus has just been betrayed, arrested, tried, and handed over to the governor to be executed. Matthew writes,

> Now at the feast the governor was accustomed to release for the crowd any one prisoner whom they wanted. And they had then a notorious prisoner called Barabbas. So when they had gathered, Pilate said to them, "Whom do you want me to release for you: Barabbas, or Jesus who is called Christ?" For he knew that it was out of envy that they had delivered him up. (Matt. 27:15–18)

Pilate has the power to release one criminal from death row. Before him is Barabbas, a notorious villain and convicted murderer, and Jesus.

> Now the chief priests and the elders persuaded the crowd to ask for Barabbas and destroy Jesus. The governor again said to them, "Which of the two do you want me to release for you?" And they said, "Barabbas." Pilate said to them, "Then what shall I do with Jesus who is called Christ?" They all said, "Let him be crucified!" And he said, "Why, what evil has he done?" But they shouted all the more, "Let him be crucified!"

So when Pilate saw that he was gaining nothing, but rather that a riot was beginning, he took water and washed his hands before the crowd, saying, "I am innocent of this man's blood; see to it yourselves." And all the people answered, "His blood be on us and on our children!" Then he released for them Barabbas, and having scourged Jesus, delivered him to be crucified. (Matt. 27:20–26)

The Crowd's Suicidal Cry

It's envy and hatred and ignorance. How could they be so deceived and manipulated and corrupt to give the *Son of God* over to death and spare a known murderer? Pilate knew that what they were demanding was wrong, that Jesus was innocent. He wanted no part or role in his execution. But *these people*, filled with unbelief, with rebellious hearts, with envious rage against their own Messiah, cried, "Crucify him! Crucify him!" "Pilate, if you won't kill him, *let his blood be on us!*"

Let his blood be on us? Let the blood of God himself be on you? Let the blood of the eternal living and creating Word be on *you*? Their unbelief and their jealousy—their sin—led them to the ultimate act of defiance and rejection of God. They crucified his Son, the Promised One—the Son he had sent to save them from centuries of unfaithfulness. *Let his blood be on us!*

The Sin That Nailed Him There

This is sin, to reject Jesus, to declare he is nothing but a delusional or deceitful man. And this was the condition of our heart, when filled with unbelief, we rejected God, his Son, and his sacrifice. *We* have screamed, "Crucify him!" with our unfaithfulness and disobedience. We have said with the crowd, "He is not our King!" "He is not our Messiah!" "Let his blood be on us!"

But God, being rich in mercy and being patient with us, his chosen people, "has shone in our hearts to give the light of the knowledge of the glory of God in the face of [this crucified] Christ" (2 Cor. 4:6). And being alive by faith in him, we *cling* to the cross on which our Savior died. It is by his precious blood that we are forgiven and freed from sin and its consequences.

Same Cross, New Cry

So, now, we say with an entirely different meaning, *let his blood be on us*, not *defiantly* as the crowds that crucified him, but *desperately*—with gratitude and hope and adoration—as those who depend wholly on his sacrifice. *Jesus, let your blood be on us. Let it cover us. Let the blood that flows from your head, your hands, your feet wash over us and cleanse us from all of our iniquity.*

We proclaim Jesus's death. We rejoice in his death, *not* because we believe he was a fraud or a lunatic, but because it is by his death, by his wounds, *by his blood* that we are healed.

EVENING

HE DESCENDED INTO HELL?

Joe Rigney

Joseph bought a linen shroud, and taking him down,
wrapped him in the linen shroud and laid him in a
tomb that had been cut out of the rock. And he rolled
a stone against the entrance of the tomb. (Mark 15:46)

We all know that Jesus died. "'Father, into your hands I
commit my spirit.' And having said this, he breathed his
last" (Luke 23:46). But what happened after he died? We
know that his body was laid in Joseph's tomb, but what
about his human soul?

Reflecting on this question not only sheds light on the
Bible's teaching about death and the afterlife, but it also
is a great encouragement to us, who must face death and
seek to do so without fear.

What Is Death?

First of all, what exactly is *death*? Death is separation, a dividing of things that ought to be united. Fundamentally, it is separation from God. Paul suggests as much in Ephesians 2:1: "You were dead in the trespasses and sins in which you once walked." To walk in sin is to be dead, to be enslaved to dark powers, to be separated from God, to be children of his wrath. This type of separation is an estrangement, a hostility, an alienation from the life and hope of the living God. In this sense, all of us, by nature, are born dead, and it is this death that Jesus endured in his suffering on the cross.

But of course, death is more than just separation from God. Death also marks the separation of the soul from the body. God made human beings to be embodied souls and ensouled bodies, and death rips this union asunder. But what happens to these two parts after they're separated? Psalm 16:10 gives us a window into the biblical teaching.

You will not abandon my soul to Sheol,
or let your holy one see corruption.

This passage directs us to the normal account of what happened when a human being died prior to the death and resurrection of Jesus. The soul was abandoned "to Sheol," and the body saw corruption or decayed.

In Acts 2:29–31, Peter tells us that David, in writing this psalm, foresaw the resurrection of Christ, "that he was not abandoned to Sheol (that is, his soul wasn't), nor did his flesh see corruption" (notice that Peter reads the second line as a reference to Jesus's body or flesh). Thus prior to Jesus, at death, souls normally went to Sheol, and bodies (flesh) decayed. We're all familiar with the latter, but the former is more opaque. A quick Bible study will show us why Peter thinks that David's prophecy in Psalm 16 is such good news.

What Is Sheol?

In the Old Testament, Sheol is the place of the souls of the dead, both the righteous (like Jacob, Gen. 37:35, and Samuel, 1 Sam. 28:13–14) and the wicked (Ps. 31:17). In the New Testament, the Hebrew word *Sheol* is translated as *hades*, and the description of Sheol in the Old and New Testament bears some resemblance to the Hades of Greek mythology. It is under the earth (Num. 16:30–33), and it is like a city with gates (Isa. 38:10) and bars (Job 17:16). It is a land of darkness, a place where shades, the shadowy souls of men, dwell (Isa. 14:9; 26:14). It is the land of forgetfulness (Ps. 88:12), where no work is done and no wisdom exists (Eccles. 9:10). Most significantly, Sheol is a place where no one praises God (Ps. 6:5; 88:10–11; 115:17; Isa. 38:18).

In the New Testament, the most extended depiction of the afterlife is found in Luke 16:19–31. There we learn that, like the Hades of Greek mythology, the biblical Sheol has two compartments: Hades proper (where the rich man is sent, Luke 16:23) and "Abraham's bosom" (where the angels carry Lazarus, Luke 16:22). Hades proper is a place of torment, where fire causes anguish to the souls imprisoned there. Abraham's bosom, on the other hand, while within shouting distance of Hades, is separated from it by a great chasm (Luke 16:26), and is, like the Greek Elysium, a place of comfort and rest.

While much mystery remains, the picture begins to take shape. All dead souls go down to Sheol/hades, but Sheol is divided into two distinct sides, one for the righteous and one for the wicked. The righteous who died prior to Christ dwelt in Sheol with Abraham, and though they were cut off from the land of the living (and therefore from the worship of Yahweh on earth), they were not tormented as the wicked were.

Where Did Jesus Go When He Died?

What, then, does this tell us about where Jesus was on Holy Saturday? Based on Jesus's words to the thief on the cross in Luke 23:43, some Christians believe that after his death, Jesus's soul went to heaven to be in the presence of the Father. But Luke 23:43 doesn't say that Jesus would be in the presence of God; it says he would be in the presence of the thief ("Today *you* will be *with me* in Paradise"), and based on the Old Testament and Luke 16, it seems likely that the now-repentant thief would be at Abraham's side, a place of comfort and rest for the righteous dead, which Jesus here calls "Paradise."

Following his death for sin, then, Jesus journeys to Hades, to the City of Death, and rips its gates off the hinges. He liberates Abraham, Isaac, Jacob, David, John the Baptist, and the rest of the Old Testament faithful, ransoming them from the power of Sheol (Ps. 49:15; 86:13; 89:48). They had waited there for so long, not having received what was promised, so that their spirits would be made perfect along with the saints of the new covenant (Heb. 11:39–40; 12:23).

After his resurrection, Jesus ascends to heaven and brings the ransomed dead with him, so that now Paradise is no longer *down* near the place of torment, but is up in the third heaven, the highest heaven, where God dwells (2 Cor. 12:2–4).

Now, in the church age, when the righteous die, they aren't merely carried by angels to Abraham's bosom; they depart to be with Christ, which is far better (Phil. 1:23). The wicked, however, remain in Hades in torment, until the final judgment, when Hades gives up the dead who dwell there, and they are judged according to their deeds, and then Death and Hades are thrown into Hell, into the lake of fire (Rev. 20:13–15).

Good News for Us

What implications does this have for Holy Week? Christ's journey to Hades demonstrates that he was indeed made like us in every way. Not only did he bear the wrath of God on our behalf; he endured death, the separation of his soul from his body. His body was in Joseph's tomb (Luke 23:50–53), and his soul was three days in Sheol, in the heart of the earth (Matt. 12:40).

But as Psalm 16 makes clear, Jesus is not only like us, but different. Jesus's body was buried, like ours, but it did not decay. Jesus's soul went to Hades, like the Old Testament saints, but wasn't abandoned there. God raised him from the dead, reunited his soul with a now-glorified body, so that he is the firstfruits of the resurrection harvest.

And this is good news for us, because those in Christ now bypass the land of forgetfulness, where no one praises God. Instead, when we die, we join with the angelic choir and the saints of old to sing praises to the Lamb who was slain for us and our salvation.

The Lord is risen. The Lord is risen indeed.

EAST
ER

SUN
DAY

HAVE YOU FOUND WHAT YOU'RE LOOKING FOR?

Tony Reinke

Like children scattering around a yard for Easter eggs, you and I are on a hunt.

We all hunt. Our thirsty souls rummage through every nook and cranny of this world, in search of shiny pleasures and saccharine delights.

Every such joy seeker, in pursuit of treasures that will not fade or rust or break or be stolen, must pay careful attention to Easter—not with a nod-off-through-the-sermon kind of attention, but with a real, earnest, eager attention riveted on Christ. If we miss the significance of the resurrection, we scamper past the greatest joy in the universe.

The Joy of Jesus

As the dark shadows stalked the soon-to-be crucified Christ, he turned his attention to joy. Throughout this Holy Week of his crucifixion, Jesus had foreshadowed his death for his disciples who struggled to make sense of it all. He addressed their concerns directly in John 16:19–24.

> *Jesus knew that they wanted to ask him, so he said to them, "Is this what you are asking yourselves, what I meant by saying, 'A little while and you will not see me, and again a little while and you will see me'? Truly, truly, I say to you, you will weep and lament, but the world will rejoice. You will be sorrowful, but your sorrow will turn into joy.*
>
> *"When a woman is giving birth, she has sorrow because her hour has come, but when she has delivered the baby, she no longer remembers the anguish, for joy that a human being has been born into the world. So also you have sorrow now, but I will see you again, and your hearts will rejoice, and no one will take your joy from you.*
>
> *"In that day you will ask nothing of me. Truly, truly, I say to you, whatever you ask of the Father in my name, he will give it to you. Until now you have asked nothing in my name. Ask, and you will receive, that your joy may be full."*

We rewind Holy Week to hear Jesus forecast the changes to come in his resurrection. He wanted his disciples to anticipate Easter Sunday as the cataclysmic dawning of true joy. And here's what it all means for joy seekers.

A Blood-Bought Joy

Jesus spoke of this joy as he faced the torture of Good

Friday. He faced denial, faced betrayal, faced beatings, faced splinters and nails and spears—he could not stop talking about joy! Only joy would keep him going. Joy was on his mind, joy was on his tongue, and joy was drawing him, not away from suffering, but *into* it (Heb. 12:2).

Jesus went to the cross for joy: to buy joy, create joy, and offer joy.

As the world celebrated the savage killing of God, out of this sea of foaming rebel hostility emerged a blood-bought, inextinguishable joy.

An Unbreakable Joy

If the killing of the Author of life could not extinguish this joy Jesus speaks about, nothing can—and nothing ever will. No opposition from the world, no opposition to the gospel, and no cultural despising of Christ will overcome the resurrection joy of Jesus.

As we have seen this week, the unquenchable joy of Easter was birthed in the greatest trauma and tragedy and evil the world has ever unleashed—the murder of the Son of God. Death, the Devil, demons, and the coordinated rebellion of mankind all allied together cannot stymie this joy. Persecutors cannot steal this joy away. No power, no event, no enemy, can sequester the resurrection joy of Jesus Christ that burst out of the tomb with him.

Worldly joys are brittle in comparison. Sickness and poverty crumble joy, and the long process of aging and dying slowly strips life of all its worldly pleasures (Eccles. 12:1–8). Death recedes all our joys, save one. Only one joy cannot be thwarted by death, because only one joy was purchased by blood.

A Newborn Joy

The resurrection joy of Jesus escapes the clutches of death because it's the joy of the new creation, a joy broken free from the evil of this fallen world.

And this makes Easter breathtaking. As Jonathan Edwards boldly declared: "The resurrection of Christ is the most joyful event that ever came to pass."[4] And rightly did Charles Spurgeon say: "No man shall ever take from me the joy that Christ rose from the dead."[5] The resurrection is the most joy-filled divine event in biblical history worthy of our eternal adulation and awe and wonder. But it's more than a breathtaking historical spectacle.

Jesus employed a common birthing analogy to introduce a radical cosmic birth. His death was the birth pangs of a new creation; his resurrection was the arrival of a new creation into history. In his resurrection, Jesus set in motion an unstoppable chain reaction that will one day culminate in the resurrection of the dead and the renovation of all creation.

Here's the point. In the long history of joy in this fallen world, after ages of unsatisfied appetites and hunger pangs in the hearts of men and women and children, the resurrection of Christ marks a crescendo. Never has joy found greater expression on earth. In John 15:11, Jesus offered his disciples "full joy," an invitation only possible from *within* the final stage in cosmic history. Such a stage was born on Easter morning.

---

4 Jonathan Edwards, *The Works of Jonathan Edwards Vol. 1: A History of the Work of Redemption* (Bellingham, WA: Logos Bible Software, 2008), 585.

5 Charles Spurgeon, "Joy in Place of Sorrow," preached 11 July 1897 at the Metropolitan Tabernacle, Newington, England, available online at http://www.spurgeongems.org/vols43-45/chs2525.pdf.

Jesus wants his disciples to thirst for a post-resurrection joy as the arrival of a newly amplified joy, a long-awaited and long-anticipated joy, a never before fully seen or experienced joy in human history. The resurrection of Christ will bring the most spectacularly joy-filled event *because* it ignites an eternally abiding and forever unconquerable joy.

The Old Testament foretold of this joy, the birth of Christ announced this joy, Holy Week seemed to extinguish this joy, but the resurrection of Christ is the point in history when the unassailable torch of God's joy emerged from the sea of foaming rebel hostility, rose up and lit the summit of an Olympic torch of joy that will burn for all eternity.

A Joy for the Asking

But as magnificently as this joy entered the world in this defining moment in cosmic history, this joy presses close to us. So Jesus taught his disciples to ask and seek for more of this joy. This is the open invitation of the Messianic age.

And this joy makes sense of the logic of John's Gospel. Jesus said he must die and go to the Father, and would leave his joy with the disciples. Once he was with the Father, Jesus sent the Spirit to dwell in them (another unmistakable sign of the new creation). United to Christ, the disciples would now pray by the Spirit, to the Father, through the Son.

Easter reshapes prayer, spirituality, and joy. With this inauguration of a new creation, the disciples became adopted sons who could pray to a Father who is eager to pour out spiritual flourishing upon them in every way, leading to a full and satisfying joy which nobody can take away.

Which is great news for the disciples.

Inexpressible Joy for You

But Jesus's bold resurrection joy promised to the disciples in John 16:19–24 is now offered to you and me. We are promised the same "joy that is inexpressible and filled with glory" (1 Pet. 1:8).

In Christ, God delights to pour out this resurrection joy into your life, a joy that fills, and a joy that cannot be stolen from you. What do we do? We simply ask our gracious Father for more of it!

The Easter joy Jesus foretold has arrived, and it's deeply personal. The resurrection is both a cosmic event, and it comes intimately close, reminding us of God's work in our lives. "The point of Easter is that God is in the process of clearing this world of all heartbreak" (John Piper). Therefore, "Christ's resurrection not only gives you hope for the future; it gives you hope to handle your scars right now" (Tim Keller).

Such a restoring and reviving joy was purchased for you and me in the resurrection of Christ.

Feast and Celebrate

Easter is for stark contradictions.

If Christ is still dead, death reigns, and all our joys are vain. So hoard every plastic Easter egg you find, because whatever you find inside is all the joy you have to grab. Or, as Paul says, "If the dead are not raised, 'Let us eat and drink, for tomorrow we die'" (1 Cor. 15:32).

But if death is dead, and if the dead are raised—if Christ is risen from the dead!—brothers and sisters, let us feast and celebrate, for the dawning light of our inextinguishable and inexhaustible eternal pleasures have broken into the darkness, offering us a life of joy in Christ that cannot fade or rust or be stolen away!

Today, delight in the resurrection joy of Christ, pray it bigger in your life, and treasure it for all eternity.

THE TRIUMPH OF JOY

David Mathis

> *"Do not be alarmed. You seek Jesus of Nazareth, who was crucified. He has risen; he is not here. See the place where they laid him." (Mark 16:6)*

The word on the street that Sunday in the Holy City was almost too good to be true. This was so unexpected, so stupendous, such a dramatic reversal of the heartbreak and devastation of the previous three days. This would take days to sink it. Weeks even.

In some ways, it would take his disciples the rest of their lives to grasp the impact of this news. *He has risen.* Indeed, for all eternity his people still will stand in awe of the love of God on display in Christ's death, and the power of God bursting forth in his resurrection.

The Sheep Had Scattered

No one truly saw this coming, except Jesus himself. He

told his disciples plainly that he would be killed, then rise again (Mark 8:31; Matt. 17:22–23; Luke 9:22). He had hinted at it as early as the first temple cleaning (John 2:19). At his trial some testified against him that he'd made such an outlandish claim (Mark 14:58; Matt. 26:61; 27:63). Then there were his references to "the sign of Jonah" (Matt. 12:39; 16:4), and the rejected one becoming the cornerstone (Matt. 21:42).

But as much as he'd done to prepare his disciples for it, a literal crucifixion was so contrary to their paradigm that they had no meaningful way to bring it into their minds and hearts. It was "a stone of offense and a rock of stumbling" (Isa. 8:14) for the long-awaited Messiah to go out like this. His men had abandoned their master in his most critical hour, leaving him alone to carry the weight of the world's sin. And the greatest burden of all—being forsaken by his Father.

One of his own had betrayed him. The chief among his men had denied him three times. After his death, the disciples dispersed. "Strike the shepherd, and the sheep will be scattered" (Zech. 13:7). Their doors were locked (John 20:19). Two even took to the road and were on their way out of Jerusalem (Luke 24:13).

When news came from the women, it seemed like sheer fantasy. "These words seemed to them an idle tale, and they did not believe them" (Luke 24:11). It was beyond their imagination, but not beyond God. Could such a dream become reality? Might there be, after all, some deep magic that could turn back time? Better, might there be a power magnanimous enough to bring in a whole new age—the age of resurrection—and triumph over the final enemy, death itself?

Seized with Astonishment

The initial report left them in shock. Mark tells us the women "went out and fled from the tomb, for trembling and astonishment had seized them, and they said nothing to anyone, for they were afraid" (Mark 16:8). *Astonishment seized them.* Had the news been less spectacular, perhaps they would have celebrated without hesitation. But this was far too big, and too surprising, to melt into immediate rejoicing. They were stunned. That's what Easter does to the human soul when we own up to the reality of its message. That's how explosive, how cataclysmic, how *world-shattering* it is that Jesus is alive.

It is a joy too great for instant gratification. First there is utter astonishment. Then comes the mingling of "fear with great joy," and finally the freedom to rejoice and tell others (Matt. 28:8).

Sadness Comes Untrue

But what now of his passion? What of his excruciating agony at Golgotha? Yes, as C. S. Lewis says, the dawning of this resurrection age "will turn even that agony into a glory."[6] Now Joy has triumphed over sorrow. Day finally has dominion over night. Light has thrashed against the darkness. Christ, through death, has destroyed the one who had the power of death (Heb. 2:14). Death is swallowed up in victory (1 Cor. 15:54).

Easter now has become our annual dress rehearsal for that great coming Day. When our perishable bodies will

---

6 C. S. Lewis, *The Great Divorce* (New York: HarperCollins, 1946), 69.

put on the imperishable. When the mortal finally puts on immortality. When we join in the triumph song with the prophets and the apostles,

> *"O death, where is your victory? O death, where is your sting?" (Hos. 13:14; 1 Cor. 15:55)*

Just as rehearsing the details of Jesus's final days leading up to the cross prepares us for the fiery trial coming on us, so also Easter readies us for the triumph that will follow. Easter is our foretaste of glory divine.

Christ has been raised. Day no longer is fading to black, but night is awakening to the brightness. Darkness is not suffocating the sun, but light is chasing away the shadows. Sin is not winning, but death is swallowed up in victory.

More Than Conquerors

Indeed, even agony will turn to glory, but Easter doesn't suppress our pain. It doesn't minimize our loss. It bids our burdens stand as they are, in all their weight, with all their threats. And this risen Christ, with the brilliance of indestructible life in his eyes, says, "These too I will claim in the victory. These too will serve your joy. These too, even these, I can make an occasion for rejoicing. I have overcome, and you will more than conquer."

Easter is not an occasion to repress whatever ails you and put on a happy face. Rather, the joy of Easter speaks tenderly to the pains that plague you. Whatever loss you lament, whatever burden weighs you down, Easter says, "It will not always be this way for you. The new age has begun. Jesus has risen, and the kingdom of the Messiah is here.

He has conquered death and sin and hell. He is alive and on his throne. And he is putting your enemies, all your enemies, under his feet."

Not only will he remedy what's wrong in your life and bring glorious order to the mess and vanquish your foe, but he will make your pain, your grief, your loss, your burden, through the deep magic of resurrection, to be a real ingredient in your everlasting joy. You will not only conquer this one day soon, but you will be more than a conqueror (Rom. 8:37).

When he wipes away every tear, our faces glisten more brilliantly than if we never would have cried. Such power is too great to simply return us to the Garden. He ushers us into a garden-city, the New Jerusalem. Easter announces, in the voice of the risen Christ, "Your sorrow will turn into joy" (John 16:20), and "no one will take your joy from you" (John 16:22).

Easter declares, for all time, that the one who has conquered death has now made it the servant of our joy.

❋ desiringGod

Everyone wants to be happy. www.desiringGod.org was born and built for happiness. We want people everywhere to understand and embrace the truth that *God is most glorified in us when we are most satisfied in him*. We've collected more than thirty years of John Piper's speaking and writing, including translations into more than 40 languages. We also provide a daily stream of new written, audio, and video resources to help you find truth, purpose, and satisfaction that never end. And it's all available free of charge, thanks to the generosity of people who've been blessed by the ministry.

If you want more resources for true happiness, or if you want to learn more about our work at Desiring God, we invite you to visit us at www.desiringGod.org.

www.desiringGod.org

.

Made in the USA
San Bernardino, CA
14 March 2016